JACOB FAIERMAN

D0645539

VOICES
in the
SHADOWS

Stories of Undocumented
Immigrants in America

In loving memory of my grandfather, Daniel, who was an immigrant himself. You were an inspiration to me and many others.

Also, for my supportive family. Thank you to my parents, grandparents, and brother.

"It is the supreme art of the teacher to awaken joy in creative expression and knowledge."
—Albert Einstein

Thank you Mr. Stephen Mounkhall

All correspondence to:
Jacob Faierman
3612 E Tremont Ave
Bronx, N.Y., 10465
www.jfsprints@gmail.com

PREFACE

Voices can move hearts and uplift spirits. They produce a wide variety of emotions, and whether for better or for worse, they produce connections that keep society moving. Finding a voice within someone or asking them to divulge the most difficult parts of their lives stimulates conversations that have the power to inform the world. If not for these types of discussions, the public could never know of their hardships, their triumphs, or their desires. Change starts with voices that would otherwise be silent.

The stories in the following pages feature the voices of those in the shadows. Their experiences speak for themselves, and their thoughts transcend the fibers of the page. This book, a collection of diverse stories from Central and South American immigrants on a journey to the United States, seeks to convey the emotions of those who wanted their feelings recorded.

In the summer of 2018, I began working at Make the Road New York, an organization of attorneys dedicated to providing undocumented immigrants with a pathway to citizenship. Family separations had come to the forefront of national news, and I wanted to get involved in my local community in whatever way possible to help the immigrant community. My work at Make the Road became a central factor that drove me to embark on writing the book. As I met with undocumented immigrants in the White Plains area of New York, they began to tell me about their home, their marital status, their native country, and their family as part of the N-400 forms, or applications for naturalization papers, that I was tasked with filling out. Although they never delved into great detail about their lives, the bits of information they gave me about their experiences both in their former countries and in the United States were compelling, and I wanted to know more about their stories.

From the Zero-Tolerance policy of the Trump administration arose shocking pictures of suffering children separated from their parents. I felt a great deal of sympathy for the families of those involved in the tragedy. My grandfather and grandmother, who came from Argentina and Uruguay, respectively, in search of opportunity, had to deal with adversity in their journeys as well. Both were searching for better lives. My grandfather wanted to practice medicine in the United States, and coming from an impoverished family in Argentina, he was always taught the value of education. He spent days and nights in the back of his father's furniture store with a book of medicine, studying in the hopes that one day he would be able to go to the United States. My grandmother had met him by the time of his departure, and they both went by plane to the United States. Looking at the photos of the children in the newspapers and on the television, I realized these children would grow up to be people with hopes and dreams just like my grandparents, who came to the United States all because of a flicker of hope that they might find a better life in America.

In the fall of 2018, I did extensive research on the plight of undocumented immigrants and the legal requirements associated with interviewing them. My teacher guided me in this research process, and I began to think of ways to contact organizations that could connect me to people who would be willing to sit for an interview. I practiced a presentation I would make to convince the heads of the immigrant organizations to trust me with their clients. To prepare my pitch, I met with three teachers who questioned me on my proposal as if they were the head of an organization that could provide me with people to interview. They asked me about the types of questions I would ask and how I would ensure anonymity in my stories. After finding the proper release forms online, I customized them to fit the project with the help of one of my teachers. After translating the forms, I spoke with my Spanish teacher to ensure they would convey the appropriate messages. These forms explained that I would not use real names in my stories in order to protect the immigrants' identities. In the following weeks, I prepared seventy-three questions that I would ask the immigrants. Although I would stray from those questions in the interview, the seventy-three questions were essential in starting my conversations with the immigrants.

For the next few weeks, I worked on contacting different organizations which had an immigrant clientele. My father, a doctor in the Bronx, also posted a sign in his office that promoted the project. Many of his patients were immigrants, and often, my father would talk with them about setting up an interview. Within a few weeks, I organized my first interview. I recall being rather nervous. Spanish is not my native language, though I had learned to speak and read Spanish through school, and through conversations with my grandparents, I realized that interviewing someone about their life would be different from classroom lessons. The first person I interviewed only knew how to speak Spanish, and despite his calming persona, I was rather anxious. I began to go down my list of questions, and I rarely strayed from the words on the paper. When I completed the interview, I felt I had gathered enough information to write a captivating story about his trip to the United States. I transcribed the interview in its entirety, and when I finally sat down to write the story, I noticed several gaps in my knowledge of his life. I had to request another interview with him, but before inquiring again, I practiced asking follow-up questions. After numerous interviews, I significantly improved my capacity for straying from the questions on my paper. By asking further questions, I was able to delve into more personal aspects of the immigrants' lives, and as a result, I could obtain a more compelling interview.

In December of 2018, I conducted multiple interviews. In addition to speaking with immigrants at my father's office, I also contacted a local community center. I heard of the center from one of the teachers in my high school. She taught English classes at the center for Hispanic immigrants, and she graciously allowed me to make a pitch to her class about my project. Initially, I met with the director of the community center, and he asked me about the aims of the project, the protections needed to interview his clients, and the potential questions I would ask them. I provided him with all the necessary information, and once I did so, I was able to prepare a pitch to deliver to the class. Everyone in the class signed up for an interview, some more eagerly than others. I worried that some people may have felt a sense of peer pressure to sign up, so I called each person before their interview to be sure they were comfortable with speaking to me about their lives.

The next week, I attended the English classes at the community center, which began at 6 pm, and I decided to conduct short, five-minute interviews with everyone who was open to a full interview. Since there were approximately twenty people who signed up for interviews, I had to do the brief, five-minute interviews before I began to do a full interview so that I could acquire the richest stories. The questions I posed in the five-minute interviews were aimed at providing me with a general overview of their stories and backgrounds, and I used these twenty recordings to guide me in my selection process for the complete interviews, which averaged approximately ninety minutes each. When I got home, I immediately took note of each immigrant

I interviewed. Since I needed to carefully select which immigrants I would conduct complete interviews with, I wrote down the talkative nature of each volunteer. The more loquacious the person I interviewed, the more likely I was to select them for a full interview. I wanted to collect the most vibrant of stories, and those who were willing to give me the most amount of detail were the people I interviewed.

For the next few months, I focused on the writing process. I always made a practice of having an interview transcribed and ready to write up because I never wanted to be in a place where I had to wait for another interview. I needed to keep the process moving, and thus, I conducted a new interview every time I came close to finishing a story. The writing process itself was not as daunting as conducting the interviews. While writing has always been one of my favorite activities, I did feel a certain pressure to capture the stories in the most accurate manner possible, without putting my own spin on the words. I wanted to establish a similar tone as compared to the mood set by the immigrant in the interview. Since I had a recording of the interviews, I could always listen to the conversations again to help me remember the tone with which each immigrant told their story. Five of the interviews were conducted in Spanish, and one of the challenges of writing the story according to a translated transcript was keeping their expressed personality during the interview in mind. As I translated their words from Spanish to English, I had to keep a similar tone so that I would not distort their voice. I took constant note of the storyteller's volume and facial expressions and wrote this down following each interview.

The writing process occurred concurrently with the interview process. I used my research on immigration and my knowledge about asking questions to guide the project. Most of the interviews occurred in a local community center, but some occurred in my father's office in the Bronx. The experience itself has not only sharpened my writing and interviewing abilities, but it has increased my awareness of the world around me. The project has opened my eyes to the outstanding perseverance of undocumented workers in the United States. I was extremely fortunate to have the opportunity to interview these immigrants and to write their stories, which I will surely cherish for the rest of my life. Their experiences may be frightening, but the way they deal with adversity conveys praiseworthy lessons wholeheartedly worth learning.

JUANA

Impoverished, lonely, and ashamed, Juana made the arduous journey across the United States border from Mexico to pursue a brighter future. At only fifteen years old, she abandoned her family without warning to evade a life of familial hatred and to receive a greater education. Her childhood and her lifelong struggle in the United States exemplify trials and tribulations that tested her perseverance to the greatest extent.

I met Juana at approximately noon on a Saturday. The room itself was rather spacious with a single window on the back wall and two desks facing opposite directions. When she first walks into the room, she is cordial yet reserved. I assume from her concerned facial expression that although she agreed to the interview, the prospect of divulging her life story most likely seems frightening. She is fifty-three years old and rather short. When I ask her to sign the release forms for the interview, she gladly does so, but when I ask the first question, she answers in a quiet, reserved tone. As the interview progresses, she becomes more comfortable, and her volume increases. However, she never forms a smile upon telling her story. She speaks with a hint of fear, as if the memories she is recalling are coming back to haunt her.

Juana grew up in the small town of Ciclista Puebla in Mexico. Her family was impoverished, and through her attempts to gain a proper education, her family enrolled her in a school at the age of thirteen.

Her parents, both farmers who never learned to read or write, struggled to put food on the table for their eleven children. Formal education was a luxury that seemed far from the norm of the town. Her early childhood was spent working in the fields for her father. She cut grass for the animals to eat and planted corn and tomatoes in the soil. Unlike most of her peers at the school, she never had time to watch television or play with her friends. Her father forced her to work in the fields, however burdensome the tasks may have been.

Despite her enrollment in the school, Juana never felt her parents' love for her. Juana is convinced that when she was born, her father tried to give her away, but no one in the town wanted her. When she confronted her parents with the accusation, her father cited the economic concerns associated with supporting another child. According to Juana, her siblings, too, never cared for her. They did not play outside together or enjoy any laughs. Rather, her siblings, along with her extended family, mocked her for her skin tone, which was whiter than anyone's in the family. Her family incessantly called her "blanco" and ridiculed her attending school, an opportunity most of her siblings never experienced.

When Juana turned fifteen years old, her father stopped paying for her education. He cited the declining monetary yield from farming. Juana continued attending classes until the end of the semester, walking into the building barefoot. She grew out of her shoes, and her father refused to buy her any new ones. The discomfort she felt was alleviated by her engagement in learning. Juana recalls one of the most painful memories of her life being when her father stopped paying for her education. The ending of her academic life, which had only lasted two years, was one of the main factors driving her away from her family.

After years of being ridiculed and the termination of her educational opportunities, Juana decided to make the journey to the United States. Crossing the border was not an uncommon occurrence for those in her town and in the surrounding areas. Juana notes that everyone in the town knew someone who was planning to cross the border at some point during the year. One night, Juana decided to leave her house and walk to the house of a thirty-year-old man who she heard was going to cross the border. His name was Francisco. Upon arriving at his house, Juana told him she was planning to make the journey alone to the United States. He resisted, but she insisted that despite her youth, she needed to go. He tried to dissuade her with warnings about possible kidnapping and rape, but she would not listen. She stood firm in her conviction, and Francisco eventually agreed to bring Juana with him. To protect her, Francisco called Juana his niece on the journey. She would leave in the next few days, and in doing so, she would abandon her family without any farewells. She took some money from her parents' hiding spot and took off into the darkness. Juana says the last time she saw her parents was the night she met Francisco on the edge of the town with eleven others, all older men.

The town of Ciclista Puebla was not far from the border. The group of twelve walked at a slow pace, stopping for rests occasionally. One night, the group was sleeping, and three men walked up to them with knives. They demanded their rations, and upon refusing, Juana's group threatened to fight them. Juana assumes that others in her group had knives as well to defend themselves, and three men had no chance against the twelve in Juana's group. The three walked away, and the next evening, Juana arrived at the border to the town of Tijuana. The group jumped across barbed wire fencing and continued down a road to the town of San Isidro. In the town, the group gathered together and took a bus to Los Angeles, where the group stayed in a small, run-down house for two days. Francisco brought Juana to a man who could take her to Brooklyn, New York, where she would meet with one of his friends. Francisco instructed Juana to tell him she was his niece and that she needed a place to stay. Despite the possible risk of his friend refusing to help, Francisco gave Juana his instructions in a firm and confident tone. Francisco said his goodbyes to Juana as he took a large portion of Juana's money and gave it to the unidentified man, telling him to take her to the airport and buy her a ticket to Newark, New Jersey. The unidentified man took Juana on a small plane to Newark, New Jersey with two tickets that he purchased. The man himself was quite reserved, and Juana, frightened at the prospects of her future, never asked him any questions. She does not recall hearing the man speak once on their way to Brooklyn.

Upon arriving in Brooklyn, the very first thing Juana noticed about New York was the volume. There were cars in all directions on every street, and there was an overwhelming quality to all the noise. Growing up, Juana had lived in a rural area of Mexico, and she had never traveled anywhere far. When Juana arrived in Brooklyn, she had only a small sum of money. She paid for a cab to take her to the address Francisco had given her, which led her to a small house off of a highway. She was a fifteen-year-old girl in the middle of a bustling city alone. She knocked on the door and was greeted by someone who spoke Spanish just like her. She was from Mexico as well, and when Juana asked for the location of the man Francisco had told her about, the woman informed her that he had died two years ago. Juana remembers what she told the kind woman, who let her stay in her home for the next few days.

"So where are you from, Juana?"

"Ciclista Puebla, Mexico?"

"And this man, Francisco, told you to come here to find the man who used to own this house?"

"That's right. I need a place to stay. Can I please stay here?"

"You can stay for the next couple of days, but I cannot support you. I barely make enough money to live here. I do, however, know of some people from your area of Mexico. I will give you their addresses so you can ask them any questions you might have."

Juana took the list of addresses the woman gave to her, and for the next few days, she knocked on door after door, attempting to find a place to stay. She asked people who were not on the list of addresses, and she asked those who were not even from Mexico using nothing but hand signals to convey her situation. Those who understood her declined, and those who did not simply shut their doors on her face. After talking with nearly everyone in the neighborhood, Juana came across someone from her hometown of Ciclista Puebla. She did not recognize him, most likely because he came decades ago to the United States. The man allowed Juana to stay with him and his family. He had a wife, but he did not have children. The man was in his late twenties.

Since Juana could not pay the couple for her stay, she was told she would have to leave unless she could find a job. For the next few months, Juana would sleep in the hallway across from the bathroom since the bedrooms in the home were occupied. Juana remembers using the owner of the house's winter coat as a blanket while the cold floor was her pillow. The next few days, she walked from shop to shop, from factory to factory, searching for any job possible. No one wanted to employ a child, and every owner questioned her about her life, one that would force her to work. They asked where her parents were instead of negotiating a possible salary or hours. After searching for days, Juana came across a factory that made shoes. The owner of the factory, Miguel, was from Mexico as well. He employed her without asking any questions. The hours were from 8 am to 8 pm, and she would be paid eighty-five dollars a week.

After finding a job, Juana was given her own room by the couple in their home. She slept on a mattress that they bought for her, but she had to pay for her own food. Juana remembers one of the most difficult aspects of her new life was managing her money when she was merely sixteen years old. She had to divide her money in a thoughtful manner, and so, she only bought cheap food. She remembers eating only potato chips and soda for dinner every day. Juana had to pay for a bus to get to work since the drive was thirty minutes. The work in the factory was tiresome and repetitive, and she was confined in one small area for twelve hours. She never finished her schooling in the United States, despite her intentions. The realities of life in the United States were only realized after experiencing her new life firsthand.

After a few years of staying with the couple, Juana was forced to move away. The couple was expecting a baby boy, and despite openly and charitably housing her for nearly three years, they needed the room in the house for their child. Juana, now nearly nineteen, had to find a new place to stay. The couple called a few friends to ask if they could house her. In only three days, the couple said their goodbyes and took Juana to a small house in the same neighborhood. There was one owner of the house, a Mexican man by the name of Antonio, a twenty-five-year-old with a short stature and a serious demeanor. Antonio was very quiet and did not talk to her often, but Juana had a bed to sleep on in her new home.

Within three months of staying in her new home, Juana came home on a Saturday evening to an unexpected party. Antonio and his friends were playing loud music and drinking a lot. There were at least thirty people in a small home that seemed to only fit fifteen comfortably. Juana joined in the festivities, and while she was drinking a non-alcoholic beverage, she noticed her senses rapidly degrading. Someone had put a drug in her drink, and that night, Antonio raped her.

Over the next few months, she found out she was pregnant with Antonio's child, and despite attempts to keep the pregnancy a secret, Antonio found out. He began to beat her multiple times a week over little arguments, and despite these despicable actions, he forced her to marry him. At nineteen years of age, Juana had one child and a husband, and the abusive relationship festered for years. Antonio continued to beat her, and she had no one to comfort her. Over the next few years, she had another child. She had one girl and one boy, and both received an education in American public schools.

For the next few years, she worked at the shoe factory, but one day, she received a notice from Miguel, her boss, that she would have to leave. Miguel was concerned for her and her family that immigration was going to find them and deport them. Thus, Miguel got in contact with

a family he knew who needed a maid. Juana worked for
the family for a few years, taking care of their children,
cooking, and cleaning. She spent most of the day at the
house, and she left after dinner every night. Juana recalls
the job being quite relaxing and engaging, at least at the
start. She enjoyed working for the family, who lived in a
large home. One day, the man who she worked for, the
father of the kids she took care of, seemed aggravated
by her difficulty understanding English. The man was
annoyed at her constant response of "yes" to every
question he asked. Juana did not know much English at
the time, and because of her limited vocabulary, she felt
helpless. The man eventually started to verbally abuse
her, and one day, he attempted to take her clothes off, so
she ran away from the home as fast as possible. She was
out of a job again, and Antonio exploded when he heard
the news. He beat her for days, and she was once again
on the streets searching for a job.

She eventually came across a Mexican restaurant,
which gladly employed her. The restaurant was located
in a poorer area of the city, and when she first started,
she cleaned the dishes in the kitchen. Eventually, she
worked as a cashier in the restaurant, and finally, she became one of the chefs. At the restaurant, she developed a
passion for cooking that would stick with her throughout
her life. She cooked all sorts of Mexican cuisine, and
every day, she would sneak out some of the ingredients
to cook with at home for her children. She would work
at the restaurant for the next five years, and in that time,

she told Antonio she wanted a divorce.

Her marriage with Antonio was riddled with problems. The marriage itself was the result of rape, and the incessant beatings never stopped. Antonio did not seem to mind the idea of a divorce, as he was aggravated with Juana. The two divorced when Juana was twenty-six years old, yet she would still live in his house with the two children for the next three years until she became engaged to a new man.

Before meeting her second husband, Juana had a troubling encounter with ICE at the age of twenty-nine. After leaving her first husband, she decided to take a trip to Mexico, not to visit her family, who lived in the western side of the country while she was on the east, but rather to reconnect with her culture and contemplate her troublesome marriage. She went by car to the country, and despite the lengthy drive, she eventually arrived in Mexico. While there, she went to the local towns and visited the shops and restaurants. Juana remembers the trip as one of her most worthwhile journeys. After living in New York for over a decade, she was finally able to experience the culture she had abandoned at such a young age.

When driving back to the United States, she experienced one of the most frightening situations of her life since arriving in the United States over fourteen years ago. A young man in his twenties in a uniform approached her vehicle while she was stopping for food. He grabbed her by the arm and told her to follow him.

Juana was forced into his vehicle, which had three letters printed on its side: ICE. Juana was taken to a facility, her car abandoned in the parking lot of a restaurant, and there she was thrown behind bars. For three hours, Juana cried in agony, scared for her future. On the verge of utter panic, Juana waited until the same officer approached her again. The officer let her out of the cell and led her into a cold room with a table. Juana thought the room looked like an interrogation area, and her judgment was proved accurate. The officer began his line of questioning, which he read off of a piece of paper. He attempted to pry information out of her, asking for details regarding her crossing of the border. Juana maintained her composure and said she was always in the United States. She told the officer she was visiting family in Texas.

Juana tried to eliminate as much of her thick accent as possible so as to remain believable. The man was young, and Juana assumed that he was new on the job. After the short questioning, Juana was released. Juana was ecstatic, and she drove quickly back to Brooklyn.

She met her second husband, George, when her car broke down the following week. George, an American car mechanic, helped Juana fix her car, which was stuck on the side of the road. Juana married George a few months later, and they had a daughter together. Juana moved into George's house at age thirty, and over the next few years, as her other children were graduating from high school, she became worried about college funds. Her first daughter got into college and later went to business school on a full scholarship, and her son went off to fight in Afghanistan in the United States Army. Juana says her children are the best part of her life, and she wants to see them succeed above all else. The second husband's status as an American citizen also led her to obtain United States citizenship in a process that took many years.

Once obtaining her citizenship, Juana was opened to new opportunities. She became a cab driver, which paid well but required the necessary documents. After multiple years as a cab driver, Juana opened her own taco place, which is where she currently cooks. Her son, while in the army in Afghanistan, got into a terrible accident while parachuting out of a plane. He permanently damaged his legs, which was one of the most painful moments of Juana's life. After the accident, her son retired from the army and now takes care of the financials of the taco restaurant.

Juana and her second husband went to Mexico multiple times during their marriage. She went to buy authentic Mexican foods to cook in her taco shop, and she also carried merchandise from Brooklyn to Mexico to sell. The trips, which totaled approximately seven, occurred by car with her husband. Every six months they would leave on a Sunday and arrive on a Thursday, but approximately four years ago, when Juana was in her late forties, she and her husband had a troubling scenario that convinced them to not take any more trips to Mexico.

When they arrived in Mexico, Juana and George enjoyed the start of their stay, as they were experiencing the culture and staying in a hotel. The trip lasted four days, and when they drove back, they encountered ten men while stopping for a rest on the side of the road. These men were members of the Zeta Cartel. Juana and George protested until they pointed a gun at them, grabbing them out of the car and beating George with a bat, knocking him unconscious. The members of the cartel took Juana and George to the mountains by car; George was unconscious the whole ride. The members of the Zeta Cartel took Juana and George out of the car, beating them whenever they refused to answer a question. Juana recalls the people asking for money, but she told them she did not have any. Juana says they tortured George and herself for around six hours. Juana vividly remembers her conversation with them:

"Please release my husband. Keep me."

"Why would we do that? We need your money."

"My husband has a family, but I have no one. If you kill him, people will mourn his death. I can work for you."

"What would you do for us?"

"You can teach me to drive for you or even kill for you. I'll do anything."

Juana notes how desperate she was, but she never lost her temper. She just wanted to make a deal with them so that she and George could be set free.

"We will let you go, but we want you to bring us bulletproof vests and cartridges for guns."

"That is impossible. I can do anything else."

"Then you must bring us five-hundred dollars and clothes every month, and we will protect you in Mexico City every time you cross the border. Give us your number, and do not lie to us because if you do, we will find you and kill you."

George sat there in silence and fear as Juana bargained with the men. He did not know sufficient Spanish to communicate with them. She recalls the look of terror on her husband's face that has forever been ingrained in her memory. One of the men in the group noticed the ring on George's finger.

"What do we have here? The man has a ring. Take off your ring, and give it to us." Juana told George to take his ring off, but it would not budge.

"My husband's ring won't come off. It is not worth much anyway."

"Then we must cut it off."

"No! Please, I will do anything! Do not cut off my husband's finger! I beg you!"

George viciously attempted to take off his ring. Just as one of the men took out a pocket knife to sever his finger off, George used his saliva to slide the ring off and give it to the men. The men drove both Juana and George back to their car at the bottom of the mountains, but before letting them go, they opened the trunk of the car and confiscated nearly every asset: their computers, phones, credit cards, and documents. Juana gave them her number as agreed upon, and they told her to not say a word to the Mexican police because if they did, the Zeta Cartel had people who would catch them and kill them. Juana says even today she is waiting for a call from someone in the Zeta Cartel to ask for money. Juana notes the sheer terror of that day was one of the most scarring events for her. She had no idea what was going to happen to her, and she could only pray for her and her husband's safety.

She drove back to New York with absolutely nothing but a car, water, and food. Juana and George almost got to the border between Mexico and the United States when another gang of ten men stopped them. Juana and George tried to swerve out of their path, but they chased them down. George and Juana were mortified, and when they pointed a gun at them, Juana was forced to listen. The men were a part of the Gulf Cartel. George told them in broken Spanish their state of affairs. He said the Zeta Cartel took everything from them. Juana began to furiously cry, begging them to not kill her or George.

"Please do not kill us. Take our car; it's all we have. Please. They kidnapped us and took everything" Juana began to pant uncontrollably in a panic attack.

"Who kidnapped you?"

"The Zetas."

"Where?"

"They took us from the mountains near Mount

King."

"Where are you going?"

"New York, but we have no money or documents. Maybe you know a girl by the name of Lisa. My husband has a niece who lived in Reynoso."

"Oh, yes, the hairdresser. Ok. We will help you and protect you."

The men put their guns away and took them to a small building in their car. There, they gave Juana and George directions to New York and told them how to cross the border without their documents. They gave Juana and George food and expressed a deep concern for their well-being. Juana notes their graciousness when she was on the verge of collapse.She remembers that day as one of the most terrifying and chaotic days of her life.

Juana's life of pain, fear, and neglect started from the moment she was born. Her struggle with her family resulted in the abandonment of her culture and lifestyle at the young age of fifteen. Her life in the United States was no less forgiving as she struggled as a victim of homelessness, rape, abuse, and violence. Her story was not clear-cut, as she did not simply travel to the United States never to return to Mexico. Her multiple visits back to her homeland while living in Brooklyn showed her determination to reconnect, despite the dangers of such trips. At the age of fifty-three, the product of her devotion to her children shines in their accomplishments, fighting for our country and attending well-respected universities. These achievements seem like unfathomable fantasies in comparison to her childhood of ridicule and financial disrepair. Juana looks forward to a future with renewed hopes vested in the success of her children.

MATEO

Sometimes escaping a life of torment requires one to go through a journey of hell. Mateo, a high school graduate from Guatemala, was forced out of his country in search of a better life in the United States fourteen years ago. In his early twenties, Mateo embarked on a trip that would test his willpower, both mentally and physically.

I arrived at the community center before English classes began. After hearing about my plan to collect interviews from immigrants, Mateo gladly agreed to be interviewed. He regularly attended language classes in the center, which contributed to his sense of security when the interview began.

We both sit at a large wooden table with plastic chairs. Mateo is wearing a heavy winter coat and a blue cap on his head. He seems to be in his early thirties. Mateo signs the release forms without hesitation, and as I begin asking questions, he becomes increasingly devoted to providing the most heartfelt responses possible. Despite interruptions from phone calls or voices from behind the divider that separates us from the language class, Mateo seems unfazed as he repeatedly presses 'decline' on his phone. Mateo is rather timid, notable in his controlled demeanor and quiet tone; although he is soft-spoken, he genuinely wants to tell his story. By the end of the interview, he is overly gracious despite the great weight his story holds.

Mateo grew up in a small town in Guatemala. He had two loving parents, a sister, and a brother. Mateo was fortunate enough to be able to attend school, and although his family struggled economically, his house was moderately-sized, and his family was tightly-knit. Every day, Mateo would wake up and ride a bike for fifteen minutes; then, he would take a train to school. His parents had always valued education for all of their children, and they wanted them to succeed to the fullest extent. Mateo's mother worked on a farm where she managed the cows, and his father worked in construction. Mateo notes that the arduous labor involved in construction often left his father exhausted by the end of the day. His father was always longing for rest, Mateo says, but his father persevered to support his family.

The United States had always been promoted as the land of opportunity in Guatemala, Mateo says, and his parents had always wanted to go to the United States to realize their goals. The instability in the Guatemalan economy and the political scene were the main factors driving the decision to make the arduous journey. Guatemala was in a state of great monetary inflation, and the United States was deemed an economic paradise in comparison. Thus, after years of saving money, Mateo's father fled to the United States, leaving his family in hopes of attaining the American dream.

The absence of Mateo's father became a reality when Mateo graduated. Mateo had been the first person in his family to graduate from high school. As Mateo looked into the audience, his mother and siblings were present, but his father was in the United States. The fate of Mateo's father was uncertain, and so, the household never felt the same, Mateo says. The family was no longer whole, and as time progressed, Mateo's family planned to send him to America so that he could meet with his father in New York. The decision would divide the family even further, yet Mateo would have opportunities to advance in society, opportunities that were not present in Guatemala.

Mateo came to the United States in August. The trip took approximately a week, yet adjusting to life in the United States would take years. When he said his goodbyes to his family, Mateo recalls feeling helpless and scared for the future. The uncertainty surrounding the trip loomed, for he knew finding his father in the United States would be a difficult challenge.

Mateo left Guatemala on his own by foot, and on one of the first few nights, he found himself in a forest with a tent. He walked into a shaded area to find shelter for the night, and in doing so, he was completely isolated from society. The only sounds he heard were those of nature. The leaves under him were rustling in the wind, and the sun was barely visible behind the canopy. The trees were enormous, and the environment was unlike any he had seen before. Mateo had grown up in a rather urban area of Guatemala, and he never had time to explore the natural world. The crisp air of the environment was refreshing, yet the uncertainty that came with his journey was unsettling. He wrestled with such emotions all night as the cicadas were humming, and the wind blowing through the branches of the trees generated an unsettling noise. Mateo remembers a howling outside his tent. A few minutes later, a wolf appeared. The prospect of dying in the woods with no one around was horrifying, Mateo says. Sheer terror overwhelmed him as he attempted to retain his composure. Before closing the tent's opening, as if doing so would make the wolf instantly disappear, Mateo could only see an outline of the wolf's body and the whites of its piercing eyes. The darkness of the night had enveloped the wolf and transformed its physique into one of monstrous proportions. After a few minutes of waiting anxiously, the wolf finally left. Mateo could not sleep all night, and in the morning, he ran as fast as possible out of the forest.

Mateo met new people soon after who were also seeking opportunity in America. He recalls the bloody feet of those around him whose shoes had been worn down. He had to walk through various towns and rural areas, and as the landscape diverged from Guatemala's topography, it became harder to navigate. Those he met, however, soon became great companions. They came from all over Central and South America. Mateo recalls some being from Mexico and El Salvador.

Mateo most notably remembers a sixty-year-old man in the group who was falling ill. The man's name was Pedro, and his worsening condition on the journey likely resulted from the summer heat. Mateo vividly recalls Pedro urging them to move forward. "Go ahead. I will be fine on my own. I will go when I can walk again. Don't worry about me."

"We want everyone who came with us to make it to

America. We are not going to leave you behind, Pedro," said Mateo.

Pedro was swept into a hallucinatory haze as he began to fumble his words. He could no longer walk, despite multiple attempts to do so. Mateo remembers dividing the group's rations accordingly, and everyone in the group worked cooperatively to make sure Pedro continued to move forward. They gave a large portion of the water supply to him, and no one objected despite concerns about their personal health.

Mateo and Pedro would both end up making it to America, despite the risks he took to ensure the group's survival. Almost everyone in the group had different views of what America had to offer, and when they arrived, each went their own way. Mateo wanted to go to America not for a rich life but for a better life. He wanted to reunite with his father, and despite the hardships he had to face once he got to America, the journey was much more daunting, Mateo says. The most difficult part of the journey was seeing strong, independent people torn down by the pains of abandoning their families or fears of being demonized once arriving in the United States. Although the journey's physical privations were horrifying, Mateo says that the mental challenges were just as formidable.

Upon arriving in the United States, Mateo was overwhelmed with the steps he had to take to reunite with his father. Those who traveled with Mateo had all gone their separate ways, and he had only brought a small sum of money. He was unsure of exactly where he was, but as he walked along the side of a turnpike, Mateo noticed the signs that led him toward a small town. His shoes, covered with mud, were on the brink of ripping apart. His clothes were also threadbare, and despite multiple attempts to swipe the dirt off, the dust particles were already deeply embedded in the fabric. The road seemed to go on perpetually as direction signs and cars were sparse. After hours of tireless walking, Mateo finally reached a small town, which was by no means wealthy, yet it was much more so than his hometown. There were brick buildings with glass windows and gardens in the front lawns of the houses. Mateo was in awe of the material conditions of the town in comparison to that of his home. Despite the various homes around him and the multiple cars driving on the road, he could not ask for directions to the nearest bus stop. The language barrier prevented him from communicating with anyone, resulting in a feeling of despair that Mateo says remains with him even today.

Mateo followed the signs beside the roadway until he approached a bus stop. Others were waiting, all of whom were speaking English. Mateo was searching for a way to get to New York, and although his route was not direct, he finally arrived. The air was relatively warm from the summer months, but the day was darkened by overcast skies. Mateo's mother had given him an address before leaving Guatemala to an apartment complex in a small city outside of New York City, that of his father.

Mateo eagerly began searching for the address as his journey's end appeared within reach.

Mateo approached the brick building in the middle of the night. He entered through a chipped wooden door right off of a stone walkway. He walked up three flights of stairs and knocked on the door. An eerie silence permeated the air in the hallway; either few people lived in the complex or most were sleeping. A man approached the door almost in a sprint as his footsteps created loud vibrations on the wooden floor. Mateo remembers seeing his father standing there almost in an ethereal haze. His father had been a distant memory after their long separation and the troublesome journey Mateo had embarked on. His father was not only a warming presence but a symbol signifying the end of a long trek through hell, one replete with doubt and fear. The two laughed and then embraced. Mateo reports the following dialogue as going something like this:

"Mateo! It has been so long, son!"

"I missed you so much, father! I have been traveling for so long with no friends or family along the way."

"How is your mother? Is she doing well?"

"She is doing great, but she was concerned about my trip here."

"Well, there's nothing to be worried about now, son. You're here, and now we need to get you a job to make your mother proud."

Mateo and his father began conversing with utter jubilation. Mateo says that they were talking so loudly and laughing so hard the neighbors probably woke up from all the commotion. The two recounted stories the entire night, and despite Mateo's uncertainty for the future in finding work, Mateo recalls his father's sense of innocent joy for his son's future, as if arriving in the United States was a miracle and a blessing.

The very next morning, Mateo had to confront the reality of his father's economic burden. At around four in the morning, his father left the house despite talks with Mateo which had lasted into the late hours of the night. Mateo does not recall his father leaving for work since Mateo was so tired. He slept until at least nine in the morning and left the house in search of work. He walked along the unfamiliar streets and once again was confronted with a stark change in the culture around him. Those walking on the streets were speaking a different language. He could only discern what they were saying based on their facial expressions, and such curiosity drove him mad with an insatiable desire to return home. Mateo's confrontation with his new reality was chilling, and even on his first day in the United States, the nostalgia and the home-sickness he experienced was unparalleled to any he had known before. He was a ghost walking along the streets with little attention being given to him and little direction on where to search for work. His father had been working in construction back in Guatemala, and in the United States, his father had found a similar job, only he was paid much more. Mateo's father was able to afford a tiny apartment near one of the busiest cities in the world, and so long as Mateo was in his presence, his son committed himself to being a contributor, not a drain, to the financial status of this branch of his divided family.

After multiple days of disappointment, Mateo finally came upon a job opportunity at a car wash, hours from his apartment. He walked into the shop, and when he noticed an English sign posted on their window, he had assumed that the manager only spoke English. Mateo did not utter a word, and he solely used hand gestures and facial expressions to communicate. The man standing in front of him laughed hysterically as he began to speak Spanish to Mateo.

"You look ridiculous! What are you doing, friend?"

"Oh, thank goodness. I thought you only spoke English. My name is Mateo, and I was searching for a job here. The sign said job wanted."

"And just how do you know what that sign was saying if you don't speak English?"

"My father told me to search for those two words on every shop I come across. I can do anything. I can clean cars if you need me to. I can help in any way."

"Then you've got a job, Mateo."

The job offer put a smile on Mateo's face. He could not stop expressing sheer joy as he had finally found a job in America. Despite the long commute, he knew his father would be proud. Mateo finally had secure employment in the United States. He had found a job that would solidify his place in his father's apartment, and he knew that if he worked as hard as possible, he could succeed and contribute to the family.

As the winter months approached, Mateo realized the magnitude of the job he had agreed to. Contrary to his initial thoughts about fulfilling the American dream when he became employed, Mateo soon recognized the immense struggle associated with working at the car wash. He was paid hourly, but the money was often not enough to sustain himself. His father made a better living than he did, and despite attempts to get tips from the drivers who came by, oftentimes people disregarded such a request. The job required twelve-hour workdays, which was only a portion of the total amount of time the job siphoned from his day. Mateo says he had to walk for approximately two hours before arriving at the car wash every day. As a student in Guatemala, he had never been exposed to the pain of labor. His father, who had been accustomed to menial work in Guatemala, seemed to comply just fine with his daily schedule. He, along with Mateo, woke up at four in the morning and went to work. As the weeks went on, Mateo felt weights on his eyes as sleep became a rarer commodity. The winter months were especially difficult as brutal, bone-chilling cold bore down on New York. Mateo says that the first few days of frigid temperatures were especially painful, and despite the layers of clothes he wore, the cold made the job unbearable. The hours seemed to stand still, unlike in the summer months. As the years went on and Mateo became a bit older, the winter months became more dreadful to deal with. His fingers felt frozen by the end of the day to the point that he would sleep next to his heater when he arrived at his apartment.

Mateo would go on to work at the same car wash for around five years. One day, his father came home with a job opportunity for his son. "Mateo, a friend of mine, has a great job for you. It would pay more than the car wash, and you would be indoors during the winter months." The job seemed almost a miracle. Mateo would be painting houses and buildings, working for a small company. The job would be much less monotonous than the car wash, as he would travel to various buildings around the area.

To this day, Mateo still works at the painting company, and he has not seen his family in Guatemala in over nine years. He still lives with his father in the apartment, and despite Mateo's continued search for prosperity in the United States, he is taking steps that will ensure a bright future. He has begun taking English classes in a community center to overcome the daunting language barrier. Although visiting his family in Guatemala is an unclear prospect, Mateo is continuing to pursue paths of communication with his family in the hopes of one day reuniting.

Mateo's journey through hell was a product of his tenacious personality fueled by a love for his family. He faced various struggles on his journey to the United States, and even after a decade in a foreign land, many of the same problems that plagued him initially are pressing concerns today. Mateo's journey has not reached its end, and although he faced multiple failures and triumphs along the way, he is still pursuing intellectual and financial goals in the United States, a land of opportunity and, at times, pain.

CARLOS

War zones hardly ever forgive. Deafening gunfire can instantly translate into death, disability, and tears. The brightest of days morph into nightmares as friends fall and cries of agony are heard a mile away. Even the towns least expected can turn into fields of anger, and finding shelter in such a storm is often a luxury.

Carlos walks into the office holding a cane firmly in his right hand. He sits down with a smile on his face as he asks my father, "So. Dr. Faierman, I hear your son has some questions for me?" My father is a doctor in the Bronx, and although I have been in his inner office on numerous occasions, the atmosphere is rather foreign to Carlos, a long-time patient of eighty-nine years old. Usually, Carlos would go into a separate room for an examination, but today, he sits in a leather chair behind a wooden desk in a room with one window, the light shining through the glass as noon arrived. Carlos signs the interview release forms without any worries or doubts. I ask my first question, and in doing so, I begin to discover an unforgettable story . . .

Before Carlos became one of the revolutionaries, known as Constitutionalists, who believed the government had taken unjust measures to gain power, he grew up in a small town in a peaceful area of the Dominican Republic.

His family was tightly knit, mother and father acting as two enormously influential figures in his life. They often struggled economically, but however burdensome the circumstances, Carlos says, he and his family never gave up on the bonds that held their lives together. He marched forward with his life, attending school every day and helping his parents whenever possible. When raising his own children, many years later, Carlos reports that he emphasized education and family as the two central facets of life.

In his mid-twenties, Carlos met a young woman, Aliya. Their relationship developed fast, but as they grew closer, Carlos says, Aliya's father grew more concerned. Aliya was from a traditional Muslim family who disapproved of their relationship. For months, they would secretly see each other, their love growing stronger as time advanced. Carlos's family had no preference for a wife in terms of race or ethnicity. Carlos knew he had their support, but the more pressing concern was gaining the approval of Aliya's father, who explicitly expressed his disgust toward their developing relationship. Thus, Carlos and Aliya eloped, defying cultural and familial restrictions in the name of love. Aliya's father, forced to adjust his expectations for his daughter's future, acquiesced, reluctantly accepting Carlos into the family.

Needing to understand the context of this story better, I did some reading on history.com and learned that not long after their marriage, a major conflict erupted throughout the Dominican Republic. After a series of corrupt and conflicting actions within the Dominican government, factions formed and tensions raged. Juan

Bosch, the first democratically elected president of the Dominican Republic had been ousted by Elias Wessin who replaced the leadership with a three-man military triumvirate. The new leadership disenfranchised many people who demanded the reinstatement of Juan Bosch. A Civil War broke out, and the military government named people who supported their regime Loyalists.

Once the war began, Carlos immediately worried for his family. By now, Carlos and Aliya had four children. His wife and his children were both in danger, not only because of the violence on the streets but also because Carlos would soon become one of the major public critics of the government, painting a bullseye on both him and his family.

Fearing for his family's safety, Carlos visited most every family member nearby. He drove to his sister's house, telling her and her family to leave town. He went to his cousin's house to give him the same warning. The imminent danger he and his entire family were in drove him to knock on door after door, delivering the same message to his loved ones: leave now. Despite the extremity of the demand, Carlos says, the intensity of the war made the most ludicrous of circumstances seem sane. By the time Carlos rang on his parent's doorbell, they were already packing. No one knew where to go. Especially in the most secluded of rural towns, fears of war persuaded many to find shelter in an even more isolated environment. Carlos's community, once tranquil and secluded, had turned into a raging civil war fueled by indignation.

On his way back home, Carlos drove directly into a cloud of smoke. A bomb had recently hit the Duarte Bridge, and flames were shooting into the thick air from two Jeeps. Four men, two in each Jeep had been bombed, black dust covering their faces. Carlos spotted three of the men lying dead on the floor of the car, guns by their side. The dust reduced the visibility to a bare minimum, but Carlos noticed one man still breathing, motionless yet aware of his surroundings. He walked over to him, tripping on a few chunks of rock dislodged from the pavement. The concrete roads felt more like tiny grains of sand by the shore; the bomb had sent large rocks flying in different directions, splitting off into smaller pieces. A silence permeated the air; the only audible noise was the whistle of the wind pushing the dust outward.

The man had been impaled by a shard of glass from the windshield of his car. He could barely talk; only whispers flowed from his mouth. Carlos kneeled down, both his hands resting on the sides of the door covered in ash. The young man wore a badge symbolizing his Loyalist allegiance, which made him a sworn enemy to the cause that Carlos supported. "Help. Help. Hospital. Help," he whispered to Carlos in the faintest of tones. The urgency of the situation did not strengthen his voice or bolster his sense of emotion. Rather, he was fading away; his soul left his face, and in its place, a pale, ghostly complexion arose. Blood flowed from the left side of his abdomen, taking with it the last bit of life in the man's eyes. The young man was beyond saving, and Carlos heard the faint shots of gunfire in the distance. He feared being next unless he drove away with haste. He got back in his car and drove down the bridge.

As he drove farther, the sound of the gunfire, once weak in the distance, was amplified. The smoke had blinded him from seeing the tanks on the sides of the bridge. He was not driving away from the war; he was headed straight toward it. The sound of gunshots grew louder, and instead of turning around, he drove to a small library in the center of town, seemingly abandoned.

Carlos got out of his car and sprinted into the library, searching for cover as the incessant sound of gunshots stabbed the humid air in the distance. Instead of finding an empty building in which to hide, Carlos found an old man in his mid-sixties inside the library reading a text. He tilted his head upward, started directly at Carlos, and calmly said, "How can I help you?" The man gave little thought to the gunshots in the distance as if they had been normalized.

Carlos said, "I need to go to a radio station right now. Where's the nearest broadcasting center?"

The man took time to collect his thoughts, almost as if the war had not even made the slightest impact on this building, an oasis from the outside violence. Both the man and the books on the shelves seemed as they had been before the war. There was no damage in the building and no fear in the librarian's voice when he gave Carlos the address to the radio station.

The drive to the station was no less fraught with danger. Gunshots roared louder than ever before, and the dust in the roads significantly reduced visibility. The radio station was damaged from the war yet still operational. The two men at the front of the building were in uniforms, guarding the station. Carlos walked in, demanding an interview to talk about the death he witnessed on the Duarte Bridge on air. The man at the desk agreed and scheduled him to speak within the hour. The town outside the station and the station itself were nearly deserted. There were not many people available for any kind of interview in these conditions, much less someone who was willing to openly speak his mind.

Carlos knew what he was going to say. He was going to urge people to take action against the government, a powerful entity that could come after anyone who spoke out. The government often killed those who protested in public or those who challenged the legitimacy of its authority, Carlos says. After what seemed like an eternity, Carlos was called into the broadcasting room.

Carlos can still repeat the broadcast from memory. He pauses as he recites the dialogue with almost perfect clarity . . .

"Good to be with you."

"Yes, we're glad to have you here. We hear you have been in the fighting itself. How bad are the streets out there?"

"They are terrible. Fighting on both sides doesn't seem to end. I recently came across a few trucks with men inside them, all dead. They were Loyalist, defending an indefensible government. Their lives, along with countless others on both sides, will be lost unless we rise up against this corruption. I need everyone to dedicate their lives, their souls to the cause. We must stop this corruption, and we must—"

The broadcast was interrupted by screams. The interviewer started yelling at Carlos for espousing Constitutionalist viewpoints. "Do you want to get yourself killed? This propaganda is not allowed on radio stations. You should know that!" The rage in his eyes was a veil for pity. He knew Carlos had turned himself into a target. The radio station itself would survive; the government had no control over that particular station. Radio stations were always checked by the government for the passion with which guests voiced their opinions. Too strong an argument would qualify as an immediate threat to the status quo. Despite the interviewer's yelling, he sympathized with him, Carlos says, for he knew that one of his brothers was as good as dead.

Just as Carlos left the radio station, P-51 fighter-bombers soared through the skies, bombing buildings in the distance. Carlos frantically ran under a truck to shelter himself from the bombs. The fumes from both the truck and the bombs in the distance mixed to produce a thick smoky odor blocking his nostrils. A few moments later, the planes turned from the radio station.

They had bombed the buildings nearby but did not hit the station itself.

Carlos knew exactly where to go from there. He worried for his family's safety, but after advising them to move to a more isolated area, Aliya and his children were about as safe as they could be. Carlos drove to El Conde, a street in a Constitutionalist held area of the Dominican Republic. The street was home to one of the largest hotels for Constitutionalist figures, who were working to challenge the government's authority. The deputy and senators stayed there, often discussing political matters. The hotel was considered the most modern in all of Santo Domingo. The building had not been damaged in the war; the windows were clear and not a particle of dust had made its way onto the hotel. The hotel was, after all, one of the most heavily fortified Constitutionalist hotels, isolated from the fighting in the other parts of the nation.

When Carlos got to the front door of the hotel, security was present. Carlos immediately recognized one of the guards; he was exactly the man Carlos had come for. "Juan! How are you, man!" Juan was one of Carlos's close friends who worked security in the hotel. They had known each other for years before the war started. "Juan, I am in danger. I need to stay here."

"You cannot just stay here, unless of course you have saved up a lot of money, man."

"Ask your boss. Ask anyone what I can possibly do. I need to get off the streets."

"Alright, man. I'll see what I can do."

Carlos waited on the side of the road for hours. He waited for Juan to return and considered leaving since his friend had taken so long, yet he had nowhere to go. When Juan returned, he said, "Sorry for taking so long, but I have some good news. I got you a job here working security with me. You can stay here for as long as you want."

Carlos eagerly accepted the offer, making contact with his family difficult and infrequent. The days turned into weeks of standing outside a building, watching occasional cars drive by and gunshots echoing in the distance. With every shot, Carlos thought of his family, wondering if Aliya and the children were safe. Every morning, he talked with various senators staying at the hotel for brief periods of time, mainly wishing them a nice day. Although limited, connections began to form between Carlos and some prominent Constitutionalist figures.

As the weeks passed by, rumors began to spread about the government searching for certain Constitutionalists to arrest. One day, Juan approached Carlos, informing him of a threat aimed toward Carlos's life. After his speech at the radio station, the government was searching for him, possibly for arrest but more likely for execution, Carlos says. Carlos left the day after hearing about the news, but before he left, Juan gave him a parting gift. "Carlos, you have to leave the country. You have to go."

"What are you talking about, Juan? I have to go see my family right now."

"Do that quickly, but you need to leave them: your family and children."

"Juan, there is no place for me to go, and I am not abandoning my wife."

"You have to. Take this money. Use it to get to America."

"America? You've gone insane. I can't get there."

"That money should be enough, but for you only. It's all I can give you; now go quickly!"

Carlos left in the middle of the night. Carlos was driving into an isolated rural area of the Dominican Republic. For the entirety of the ride, Carlos barely focused on the dirt roads ahead of him. He was focused on the opportunity to start again in the United States. He firmly grasped the money Juan had given him. His future was in the palm of his hand.

When Carlos arrived, he ran down the dirt pathway leading up to a wooden shack with a dilapidated straw roof. He carefully opened the door so as to not scare his wife. He took off his shoes only to be met by his wife sitting in a chair. "Carlos! You have returned?" Aliya embraced Carlos for a short second as she realized the peculiarity of the situation.

"The government is searching for me. I have to leave the country."

"What?"

"I will go to the United States. Juan gave me the

money to go."

"What about us? Do I stay here with the kids?"

"I will come back once I get this sorted out. You are not in danger, Aliya; I am."

Carlos could not sleep all night. He was too focused on the life-changing decision he had yet to fully make. He knew he had to embark on the journey to America, but even hearing bombs and gunfire every day was not enough to make the decision easy.

While attempting to sleep, lights flashed outside his door. He opened the window to see government vehicles outside. "Aliya. People are outside. I need to run. Distract them. Tell them you have no idea where I am." Carlos ran through the back door into the sugarcane fields until he was breathless, the cool temperature failing to contain jolts of heat sparking from limb to limb. He was barefoot, and the shards of sugarcane and rock cut his feet. They felt like tiny needles stabbing his feet repeatedly, but his fear propelled him to run forth as fast as humanly possible. The humidity of the air made breathing difficult, and sweat began to drip down his face as he ran into the darkness. He spent that night sleeping next to the sugarcane, and when morning came, he made his way back to the house, relieved to find his children and wife were safe. "I make my trip to America tomorrow, Aliya." There were no objections.

Despite the great expense, Carlos took the first flight out of the Dominican Republic to New York. A friend he knew from the government was able to get him a three-

month visa. Once in New York, the language barrier
hit him immediately. Carlos had never spoken English
in his life. For the next few decades, Carlos would work
on learning the new language, eventually becoming
fluent. One of the most difficult struggles of his new life
was the absence of his family. Over time, he and Aliya
grew apart. One by one, the children came to America,
but after years of separation, his relationship with Aliya
had been disrupted beyond repair. The two eventually
filed for divorce as the relationship seemed untenable
with Aliya in the Dominican Republic and Carlos in
America.

There were great economic burdens in Carlos's new
home. He lived in a small apartment with little money
to support himself. Jobs seemed to come and go, and all
involved menial labor. For a few months, Carlos worked
at a construction company in New York, but one day,
Carlos had to meet with his attorney to make progress
on his status as an undocumented worker. Carlos walked
to his small apartment, which only featured a bed, stove,
and toilet, to prepare to see the attorney, but before
walking there, Carlos spoke with his boss in the construction company. "Sir, I unfortunately cannot come
in tomorrow. I have to meet with an attorney. It's very
important."

The boss, unwavering, denied Carlos's request.
"You oughta come in tomorrow, or you can kiss this job
goodbye."

Carlos stayed firm, refusing to give in to his boss's

demand.

"Fine. I will have to give up this job then, sir."

"You scum. I will report you to immigration. Get out of this place. You don't belong here."

Those words stuck with Carlos, and for years, he struggled to find a new job, but soon after he was fired from the construction company, he met his future wife. Carlos was undocumented for seven years before he attained citizenship, but despite all of the threats he received and obstacles he had to overcome, Carlos climbed up the social ladder, eventually attaining a job at the Dominican Consulate in Manhattan. He worked there for a few years, and one day, he came across a senator he recognized from the El Conde Hotel. The two men only chatted briefly, but within months, Carlos was promoted to Vice-Consul in the Dominican Consulate. Carlos attributes his success in his new job to that senator he spoke with for mere minutes in the Consulate. Carlos paved a path for himself, having two more kids and supporting a new family while also retaining connections with his four children.

War zones hardly ever forgive, but on rare occasions, they do. Carlos not only witnessed death, but he was threatened with murder for years. Standing up for his beliefs led him to a foreign land and introduced new challenges to both maintaining a relationship with his family and supporting himself economically. Not everyone has the opportunity to realize their dreams, but Carlos was able to do just that through perseverance and grit, despite being faced with numerous hurdles along the way.

JORGE

Despite his childhood experiences of relative affluence, Jorge's repeated separations from his family, now scattered across the globe, took an emotional toll on him and his children. At the age of thirty-three, Jorge made the trip to Spain from Ecuador, where he would be forced to leave behind members of his family and adopt a new lifestyle. Upon adjusting to life in a foreign country, Jorge made the difficult decision to make another challenging change: to live in the United States.

I conducted Jorge's interview in a community center, where he was regularly attending English classes. After asking the class who wanted to be interviewed, I watched as Jorge readily agreed to tell me his story. Jorge, a fifty-two-year-old man, gladly signs the necessary forms for the interview. He wears casual clothes and seems eager to begin the questioning. We are separated from the English class by a divider, and although voices can be heard from the other side, the class is relatively quiet. Jorge is focused on giving me a detailed interview, and he always maintains a serious tone while explaining his life. He is not reserved, but he is not boisterous. Instead, the interview, which begins in the late afternoon at a large wooden table, seems to be a release for him as he tells the story with sincerity and passion.

J orge was born and raised in a relatively wealthy town in Ecuador. He repeatedly mentions the privilege he possessed that not all people in Ecuador had. Jorge attended primary school, middle school, a private high school, and college. When reflecting on his childhood, Jorge notes his regrets regarding not taking advantage of his educational opportunities to the fullest extent. He was not an exemplary student, despite his parents' hopes for their child. Instead, Jorge notes that his childhood was rather sheltered. Unlike many in Ecuador, he was not concerned about his future until he grew into his adult years. He played in the streets with his friends and was rarely exposed to the economic troubles plaguing the nation at the time. Jorge says the most important person in his life was his mother, who stayed at home, imposing her moral values on Jorge that were essential to his development as a person.

Jorge's father was a hard-working man who came from a humble family. His father was not wealthy, but Jorge emphasizes his father's unwavering drive to succeed. When Jorge's grandfather passed away, his father was forced to take care of Jorge's grandmother and his grandfather's four brothers. His father went into the shoe business, and he ran a shop that supported his family while Jorge was a young boy. Jorge notes that his father's business, especially during precarious economic times, caused great stresses in the household. Jorge's family was wealthy in comparison to the rest of the nation, but their financial situation was not secure in the least.

At the age of twenty-one, Jorge met a girl in college whom he would marry that same year. When Jorge told his parents of his desire to marry, they were reluctant. They wanted Jorge to continue studying at the college with diligence, but at the time, Jorge was not concerned about his future and the role education played in paving his path toward an eventual career. He began working at his father's shoe shop to acquire the funds to buy a house. After three years, he and his wife had their first child. Jorge was twenty-four years old when his daughter was born, and he remembers that moment as one of the most impactful of his life. Jorge says that being a father changed him significantly, as he became focused on the safety and success of his child. Jorge went from what he describes as a disobedient young man to a responsible one, geared toward helping his child grow up happy and healthy. Jorge says that he gained a newfound respect for his parents when he was put into the role of a father. The next decade, however, would test him as an economic crisis hit Ecuador, sending him and his growing family into a startling new financial reality.

Jorge had three more children with his wife in his twenties and early thirties. As the economy worsened, his siblings began to leave the country. His sister and his younger brother went to Spain with hopes to succeed financially. When they were born, they lived for a time in Ecuador, but for much of their childhood, the siblings lived in Spain. The shoe business run by Jorge's father began to collapse, and his father, in desperation, started engaging in other commercial activities outside of the business. His father began to get tired and wanted to change his job, and when he offered Jorge an opportunity to buy his business, Jorge did so. The business succeeded at first, but in 1996, there was a territorial conflict between Ecuador and Peru, creating instability in the national economy. For two years, Jorge and his family depended on their struggling shoe business, which was in great debt. Jorge made the decision to close the family business and pursue a different path, which ultimately led to a separation with his wife and his children.

Jorge planned on moving to Spain, where he could pursue hopes for a better income. At the time, he justified leaving his four children and spouse by saying he was going to Spain so they could have a better life. Once Jorge had enough money and the Ecuadorian economy strengthened, he planned to return to his homeland and reunite with his family. He left Ecuador when he was thirty-three years old, and his siblings helped him with the travel expenses.

Ecuadorians did not need papers to travel to Spain at the time, and as a result, the trip to Spain was not burdened by governmental requirements. When Jorge arrived in Spain by plane, his siblings were able to get him a job in construction. Despite Jorge's lack of construction experience, the company employed him and many others from various countries around the world. After working at the construction company, Jorge began to work at a merchandise transport company. While working in both of these jobs, he formed connections with people who helped him obtain better jobs to raise his income. Jorge lived with his siblings in their apart-

ment while he paid for a portion of the rent, but he says
that when he was in Spain, he was rather lonely. The
only people he knew in the country were his siblings,
and despite their tremendous financial support and their
help searching for a job, Jorge missed his own family in
Ecuador.

For fifteen years, Jorge worked in Spain for various
companies, including those in the steel-cutting industry.
He visited his family back in Ecuador every six months
or so, sometimes for extended periods of time, yet the
separation weighed on his conscience. He wanted to return to Ecuador for good, but the financial situation was
not improving. Jorge was not rising on the social ladder,
and he was not making enough money to support both
his family in Ecuador and himself in Spain. Therefore,
he decided to go to the United States, where his oldest
daughter was living as a permanent resident. Since Jorge
had lived in Spain for such an extended period of time
with his siblings, saying his farewells to them was a
heart-wrenching experience.

Jorge described the stark contrast between obtaining
legal documents in Spain versus in the United States.
Someone from Latin America who traveled to Spain
had the opportunity to live in the country for a year, and
then they were eligible for Spanish citizenship. In the
United States, Jorge says, cumbersome legal processes
often limit immigrants from obtaining a viable pathway
to citizenship.

His daughter had already moved to the United States

from Ecuador to pursue educational opportunities three years before his arrival. Her legal status helped Jorge obtain his papers when she became a United States citizen. He explains the difficulty of the immigration process for those without citizen relatives or spouses. If his daughter had never obtained her citizenship, Jorge believes he would still be undocumented.

In the United States, Jorge was bombarded with a completely different atmosphere. Although Spain had different cultural traits compared to Ecuador, he was able to communicate in Spain, but in the United States, the communication barrier became a pressing issue. Jorge saw learning English as an essential step to obtaining a high-paying job in the United States. Jorge described the essential role his daughter played in his transition to life in the United States. She had already learned sufficient English from her time in the Ecuador school systems, and although Jorge took English classes from a community center, his daughter aided him in adjusting to the new language. Two of Jorge's children moved to the United States, and his youngest son, who was still in Ecuador, has attempted to gain entry into the country for economic opportunities.

Jorge notes that finding a job was difficult as he had to start from the lowest rungs of the social hierarchy. In Spain, he worked in various trades, but his most prominent skill was cutting steel. Jorge remembers the difficulties associated with finding a job in a similar line of work. He was forced to accept whatever job became available, regardless of his prior experience. He called his sister in Spain to help with his search, and she was able to locate relatives who pointed Jorge toward his first job in the United States. He was tasked with working for a window-cleaning company, which took a significant amount of time to adjust to. The company that employed him hired both native English speakers and those from Latin America, and thus, he was able to communicate with his co-workers most of the time.

The separation between him and the rest of his family took a significant toll on their bonds. He and his wife got a divorce after Jorge's first visit back to Ecuador since arriving in the United States. Jorge explains that his wife expected him to return to Ecuador from Spain, and when he went to the United States, his marriage fell apart. Two of his children were in Ecuador, and two were in the United States. Jorge remembers the emotional toll of the divorce and the separation from his children. His two children from Ecuador were only readily accessible by phone.

Jorge's housing situation was precarious in nature. When he arrived in the United States, he had saved funds for an apartment in the suburbs of New York. Meeting the financial requirements was a constant struggle that worried Jorge. In a few months, however, he started a relationship with another woman from Ecuador who had moved to the United States. Her uncle lived in a house in the suburbs of New York, and he gladly agreed to let Jorge stay with him. Jorge moved out of his apartment, and his fears over the rent were alleviated.

One of Jorge's most difficult times in the United States came when a destructive earthquake hit his hometown in Ecuador. Immediately after the earthquake, Jorge tried to reach his extended family back home, but they could not respond. He remembers the great extent to which sheer terror overwhelmed him. Jorge recalls thinking his family was dead, and a sense of guilt came to the forefront of his thoughts. He recalls his past decisions and his choice to not move back to Ecuador in search of economic opportunity. He regretted leaving his children for years, and he began shedding tears for his family. Jorge was not able to reach them for over three hours of calling, and when he finally got in touch with his family, they were all safe. Many of his close friends, however, had been killed in the earthquake, and his hometown was demolished. Jorge says his community had to start from scratch to rebuild both buildings and hearts.

Today, Jorge is still worried for his family. He has been in the United States for nearly four years, and he is still taking English lessons at the community center in New York. His four children are all in their twenties, and his second-oldest daughter recently became pregnant. Jorge is preparing for life as a grandfather, and despite still being separated from two of his children who live in Ecuador, he hopes to bring them to the United States in the future. Jorge's former spouse is working on obtaining legal documents to get a US citizenship with the help of her daughter, and he is still in a relationship with his girlfriend whose uncle helped him with housing. When reflecting on all his travels, Jorge recalls the difficulties of separation and adaptation. The expenses associated with travel can be intimidating, and despite attempts to regulate and stabilize an economic situation, curveballs are commonplace. Despite his wishes to see his family in Ecuador, Jorge was unable to return for eight years due to a lack of money and time from work. Once he returned, he saw his mother, his kids, and his extended family. He had always had extensive communication with them, but visiting in person, according to Jorge, is always more satisfying. Jorge firmly believes that the only obstacle preventing improvement in both his social and economic conditions is the language barrier. Over the years, Jorge received various job offers he had to turn down because they required fluency in English. Although he has attempted to learn English through classes and with his daughters, he still struggles with day-to-day conversations. Jorge often emphasizes the importance of English with his children, who were all placed into schools from a young age.

Jorge's belief that Ecuador is a country of minimal opportunity led him to explore the world in search of a more economically viable life for him and his family. Despite a heart-wrenching separation from his family, Jorge obtained job opportunities unavailable in his home country. His residencies in both Spain and the United States in a relatively short period of time reveal a hectic change in culture exacerbated by a divorce and an earthquake in his distant and unreachable home. Jorge never wanted to change his country of residence, but he was forced away from his family because of economic realities. Instead of moving back to Ecuador, Jorge is committed to living in the United States, joined by the rest of his family in the near future. His life of constant change and uncertainty underscores the importance of sacrifice and risk when faced with economic hardship.

SERGIO

Sergio grew up in a small town in Guatemala, his childhood riddled with economic difficulties. The impoverishment of his family resulted in him not receiving a complete education, and when Sergio decided to go to the United States after having three children, he experienced years of despair upon their separation. During his journey to the United States, Sergio was exposed to the terrors of crossing the border. His experiences instilled a fear and a trauma that still haunts him to this day. When Sergio finally arrived in the United States, he was forced to construct a life without his children, and only recently has he begun to put his family back together.

I met Sergio when he was taking an English class. We had organized an interview prior to our meeting, and when I arrived at around six in the afternoon, he was eager to be interviewed. Sergio and I sit across from each other with a table separating the two of us. He does not seem nervous to do the interview, and he readily signs the release papers at my request. Sergio, a forty-four-year-old, wears a baseball cap and a sweater. When I ask my first question, he answers in a confident tone, as if he had told his story about his family many times before. As I continue my questioning, he begins to talk for longer durations of time without my interruption, and his firm tone never wavers.

I n Guatemala, Sergio and his childhood family lived in poverty. Although he had many friends whom he played with frequently, Sergio only attended primary school, and he had little opportunity to study because he could not buy proper educational materials. His parents worked on a ranch growing corn, and Sergio often helped them. Economic fears were always pressing, and Sergio remembers his mother and father frequently praying for a prosperous future. His household was relatively crowded, as Sergio had seven siblings. His brothers and sisters were similarly tasked with helping around the ranch, and they too never completed their education. Many people in the area were in the same straits, and Sergio, along with his family, made many friends in church services and local gatherings, so he never felt a sense of isolation.

For the first twenty years of his life, Sergio helped his family on the ranch, and when he married his wife, he went to live in her house at the age of twenty-one. All three of their children went to primary school, like their father, but afterward, they did not receive further education until later in their lives. Instead, they worked on Sergio's family ranch. Sergio notes the importance of a proper education, and he emphasizes the necessity of learning English while in the United States.

For years, Sergio and his family continued struggling in poverty. There were few improvements in his way of life, and his family ranch barely turned a profit. His father died just after his second child was born, which caused Sergio great grief. He and his family became more responsible for helping out on the ranch, and as a result, his children had to limit their time in school. Sergio had many friends who decided to go to the

United States to seek a better life, and although he never heard from some of them again, Sergio knew he had to go. He wanted to help his family financially, and thus, he became the first in his family to attempt the trip. His seven siblings stayed in Guatemala and helped to keep the ranch stable.

Sergio, now thirty-seven years old, had three children, all of whom were receiving subpar education. He notes one of the most significant factors driving him to pursue a life in the United States was the possibility of economic prosperity so that he could help his children receive a proper education. Sergio says that at the time, he had no idea the pain that would come with separating from his family for so many years. His future was uncertain, and he never knew when he would see his family again. When Sergio said his goodbyes to his family at the ranch, he was filled with sorrow, yet Sergio explains that his despair would only get worse as the separation lingered.

Sergio embarked on his journey to the United States in June, and despite the inevitability of the extreme heat he would encounter, he figured the sooner he left for the United States, the sooner he could begin building a life of financial stability. He contacted his friends within the community who were planning to make the journey north as well. He and approximately ten others, both men and women, decided to walk together, a decision that Sergio says provided morale but hindered their safety by depleting the group of food, water, and medical supplies and by drawing attention to them.

The morning they left the town, Sergio notes the immense angst he had when seeing his family for the last time. His wife and children were devastated to see him go, and Sergio never knew when or if he would be able to return. His group met on the outskirts of the town. Each person carried a small bag of necessities, and everyone spoke with concern as they discussed their plans to move north. Sergio remembers the stuttering in everyone's voices as they tried to outline their journey. Everyone in the group seemed mentally shattered by the goodbyes they had just made. Sergio himself remained relatively quiet as others in the group took the lead. The group walked together, rarely stopping to rest. Sergio emphasizes the powerful weight of the separation between him and his family, but he says that with every step closer to America, he was closer to a better life for him and his family.

As the group walked through Mexico, they stopped in local towns to sleep. Some residents welcomed them into their homes. Sergio remembers his visit to a town in Southern Mexico where he met an older couple who gave him food, water, and a place to sleep for the night. He says their hospitality was so gracious, but in other towns, he and his group were forced away. The threat of some of the townsfolk never developed into conflict, but those who prodded Sergio and his group out of their neighborhood, ordinary citizens who threatened to call the authorities, expressed rage over their arrival in the town.

Two weeks into his journey, Sergio and his group faced what seemed to be an insurmountable obstacle. In the distance, a dark blue image was visible. As they approached, the image became clearer and clearer until everyone realized their imminent danger. Roaring rapids raged in a large river ahead of them, and Sergio and his group began to panic. For hours, the group mulled over their options, and although Sergio was worried, he recommended the group go back to the previous town to purchase a raft. They agreed, and since Sergio thought up the idea, he led the charge into the town. Sergio went to a small raft vendor on the outskirts of town, but the rafts he sold seemed to be on the verge of collapse. The dilapidated plastic seats and the chipped motor were beyond repair and refurbishment, and when Sergio approached the rest of his group and showed them the boat he was planning on buying, Sergio warned them of the faults of the vessel while also advocating its purchase. The boat was small, and the ten people in his group would barely fit on it. The group had no choice, however, and so, they bought the boat for a relatively low price.

Sergio and his group approached the rapids with the boat propped up on their shoulders. He remembers sweating profusely in the scorching heat. His vision was partially blurred as dehydration impaired his senses. Sergio notes the ferocious nature of the rapids; the force seemed as if it would topple over their raft. His group put the raft in the water, one member of the group anchoring the boat to land, and when the raft was filled to its maximum capacity, only seven people could fit. Those left onshore were anxious, and soon, everyone began to panic. Each of the remaining people in Sergio's group sat on the edges of the raft, holding onto the plastic seat on the inside. The last person on the raft had nowhere to sit, so she laid down on the floor as others moved their feet so as to not step on her. The raft was on the verge of toppling over when the person anchoring the boat let go, and Sergio along with another person on the other side of the raft used a paddle to direct the raft to the other shore. Everyone was in a panic, frantically screaming as if the volume of their yells determined their fate. Sergio remained quiet as he focused on paddling. He never stopped moving the paddle, and he began to flail the paddle back and forth, occasionally not even touching the water. He was in an inaudible panic, but he had to assert reassurance so that the others would not panic. Someone on the raft fainted, and ten seconds later, another person fainted. Everyone on the boat gasped, and as they fell over, the raft began to topple. Sergio had to push his body upright so as to prevent the boat from capsizing. They eventually reached the other shore, and Sergio had to haul the two people who fainted onto the grass. The thirty minutes they had spent on the raft felt like an eternity. Sergio never found out what happened to the three people they left onshore.

The walk to the border was only a few days from the

rapids. As Sergio and the group approached the border, one of the people in the group contacted a coyote, a person who is paid to direct immigrants across the border, to arrange the crossing. They had to wait for two weeks in a nearby town for the coyote, and they had to turn to those in the town for food and water. Sergio remembers thinking of his family during the two-week respite. He had no way to contact them to let them know he was in good health, which ate away at his conscience. Once the coyote arrived, Sergio and his group were able to cross the border, and from there, everyone split into their own groups. Some went west, but Sergio wanted to go northeast, which left him with two other people from his original group who joined him on the remainder of his journey.

When the three of them walked into Texas, they were confronted by a vast desert that featured a small road with no cars. They brought with them a tremendous amount of water so as to prevent dehydration as they began the seven day walk to Houston. Sergio remembers the monotonous nature of the desert; its sameness was blinding, and the heat furthered his suffering. The three of them slept in a small tent one of them had bought before the trip. Sergio notes the cool temperature of the night stood in stark contrast to the blistering heat that radiated from the sand during the day. They walked for hours, sweat pouring down Sergio's forehead. There was no one nearby to help them complete the trip. One day, Sergio remembers a strange cloud formation developing in the distance, an aberration from the typically clear skies. Within a few minutes, droplets of water began falling from the sky; a storm was brewing. The three of them remained calm and set up a tent to wait out the rain, but as soon as the storm began to pick up, Sergio noticed a horde of insects bursting from the sand. Ants, flies, and spiders were crawling in the thousands across Sergio's shoes, and soon, scorpions appeared from the sand. He and the remainder of his group were terrified as they darted into the tent. The storm continued to rage as the animals ran across the cold sand. One of the poles that supported the tent collapsed, which forced Sergio to prop up the roof with his hands as the incessant hissing of the scorpions stimulated a response similar to nails on a chalkboard. Sergio was in desperation, on the verge of bursting out in tears like the two others in his group had already done.

The storm lasted into the night, and Sergio barely slept. He continued walking in the desert, sleep-deprived and anxious. Scarred from the horrors of the other day, Sergio responded with sheer terror as he encountered a rattlesnake in the middle of the road. He and his two companions had to walk around it in a calm fashion so as to avoid any confrontation with the poisonous crea-ture. The rattlesnake was Sergio's final obstacle in his journey to his first major American city.

When the group of three arrived in Houston, they all split in separate directions. Sergio had plans to go to New York, where a friend from his childhood in Guatemala was situated for eight years. He used the small amount of money he had left to purchase a bus ticket to New York, and when he arrived, he immediately went to the house of his friend. For a year, Sergio stayed with his friend in his house. His friend provided Sergio with money to pay for food while he was searching for a job on the condition he would pay the loans back.

Sergio commenced his job search by speaking with others in the community. He went door to door, asking people if they had any connections to anyone who was interested in hiring. The community in which his friend lived was mostly Hispanic, and so Sergio had no issues communicating. In only one day of job searching, Sergio came across a man who worked for a contracting business in Westchester County, New York. The man was informed by his boss that they were currently hiring, and he offered to commute with Sergio on his trips to the job site. Sergio remembers the sheer jubilation he felt upon receiving his first job in the United States. He felt as if the land of opportunity he had been in search of had finally been realized. The contracting job was not tedious in the slightest, and Sergio was buoyed by the relatively large wage he received, which catapulted him into a new lifestyle. He was finally able to buy his own apartment, a luxury he previously had not experienced.

As Christmas approached, however, Sergio fell into a deep depression. With no one to comfort him, Sergio could only call his wife and children during their festivities. He was forced to sit on his couch during a cold winter night and think about the life he used to have in Guatemala. Sergio, in a state of despair and solitude, spiraled into a state of mental anguish and regret. For the next few months, Sergio contemplated going back to Guatemala, but the trip was impossible. For two years, Sergio barely budged on the social ladder as he continued working six days a week for the contracting company. Christmas of the next year, his eighteen-year-old son, Jose, called to tell him he intended to make the journey to the United States to reunite with his father and start a new life. Sergio was appalled and quickly disapproved of Jose's plans. He firmly argued against Jose, who contended that since his father had survived the trip, he would surely do the same. Sergio was in a state of disbelief as his yells were unpersuasive to the impermeable tenacity of his child.

For a month, despite repeated pleas not to come, Jose walked toward the United States in a group not dissimilar to the one his father had traveled in. Sergio remembers the countless days of sleepless nights he suffered during Jose's journey. Communication between him and Jose ceased as cell phone usage was not available. His son was on his own, and Sergio had no way to know whether or not Jose was safe. Sergio notes that these days were amongst the most worrisome in his life. Every night he prayed for his son's protection from the hazards of the journey. He incessantly called his wife by phone, hoping she or anyone in the town had heard about Jose's whereabouts. Sergio knew the trip took a significant amount of time, but he never expected his son would travel alone on such a dangerous journey. Jose eventually made it to New York, and the night of his arrival, he told his father about his trip. Unlike his father, his group stuck together during the entirety of their journey, and they would have come into contact with immigration officers had it not been for one of the members of his group who knew where the officers were stationed. Sergio says his son experienced a less treacherous journey than he did, and he attributes his attentiveness in prayer to Jose's safe return.

Sergio managed to get Jose a job in the same contracting company he was working for at the time. Sergio began to attend English language classes to hopefully rise on the social ladder and attain a better-paying job. Sergio is still taking these classes, and recently, he acquired a new job in landscaping, which offered a higher salary. He and his son now both live in an apartment, and Sergio hopes that his daughters can one day come to the United States in a safe and legal fashion once they complete their education. Sergio hopes he can continue to prosper in the United States but recognizes the uncertainty of his future in America given his lack of papers.

⊢――――――――――――――――――――――――⊣

Sergio's faith in the American Dream compelled him to embark on a treacherous journey to the United States. Along with the mental anguish of abandoning his family and friends, Sergio confronted physical threats to his life. From paddling against rapids on a rickety vessel to trekking through a desert as scorpions and snakes arose from the sand, Sergio encountered dangerous scenarios that made him doubt his journey. The precarious economic situation in Guatemala eventually drove his child out of the nation as well, and despite the prospect of reuniting with Jose after a lonely few years in the United States, Sergio was forced into a state of anxiety for months as his son's future was not a guarantee. Sergio will hopefully reunite with the rest of his family in the near future as he prays for the success of his two daughters, still separated from their father in an increasingly beleaguered relationship.

ADRIANA

Adriana came to the United States curious as to what her future would hold. At only five years of age, she knew little of the forces that were propelling her out of Guatemala. She placed her trust in her mother, who would guide them on their trip and provide them with the educational tools necessary to succeed in the United States.

I met Adriana at 5:30 pm in a Starbucks. We had arranged to meet prior to the interview, and she had already been briefed on the aims of the project. She was eager to tell me about her life, perhaps because of her youthful alacrity. She was a mere nineteen years of age, but she spoke with sophistication and grace, likely as a result of her vast educational background. We sit down at a table in the back of the coffee shop, and I purchase her a cold Strawberry Acai Refresher, which may relieve some of her angst. She does not seem beleaguered by the trials and tribulations she has faced in her life. Rather, she signs the legal papers and tells her story constantly smiling as if the nostalgia of her youth is interlaced with her words.

A driana's memories of her childhood in Guatemala were rather hazy, as she only lived there for the first five years of her life. Her memories in her home country are confined to the simple pleasures of life with her extended family. Adriana and her cousin would always speak with their great grandmother as they helped her pick peas in the garden. The stories her grandmother told were of past generations and their struggles, and although Adriana could not remember their specifics, she recalls their adventurous nature. She and her cousin also used to sneak out of the house during the day and go to the stores. One day, she and her cousin were absent from the familial affairs for an extended period of time, and everyone began looking for them, finding them eventually.

Every day, the school teacher would pass by Adriana's house, but Adriana's family could not send her to school. Eager to attend classes, Adriana implored her mother to enroll her in the school system, but there was no feasible way to attend school while in Guatemala. Adriana had to help her family in the gardens, and the financial strain of pre-school was not worth the struggle.

The economic pressures of life in Guatemala were exacerbated by a horrible accident involving Adriana's father. Adriana's grandfather owned a transportation company that took people from Guatemala City to the surrounding towns. Her father, who was one of the bus drivers for the company, was on his way back into Guatemala City when he got into an accident. By God's grace, Adriana says, nobody died, but the drivers' side of the bus was crushed. Adriana's grandfather demanded his son pay the money back to replace the damaged bus, but he did not have the necessary funds to pay for the new bus. For a few days, Adriana's mother and father talked over their options. They had wanted to go to the

United States since they had been married, and now, there was reason to leave. Adriana's father devised a plan to travel to the United States alone to earn the money for the bus. After paying back his father in law, he would travel back to Guatemala to reunite with his family.

When Adriana's father left, his future was uncertain. The extended family was concerned for his well-being, especially since he was traveling to the United States on foot. For weeks, Adriana noticed her mother fall into a state of desperation. She was mourning the separation, and after two months of contemplation, she made the choice to travel to the United States so that their nuclear family could remain whole. Taking a five-year-old Adriana and her eight-month-old baby brother, Adriana's mother made a decision that could have been the end of her family. She knew her husband had settled down in New Jersey, but navigating the journey to America with little funds and two young children would be difficult. Her extended family begged them to stay in Guatemala, concerned about the dangers of starting a new life in a foreign country, but the prospect of reuniting with her husband fueled her decision. Some in the family suggested leaving her eight-month-old baby in Guatemala, but then the infant would grow up in a world without his mother, father, and sister.

They began their trip to the United States by taking a plane to Texas, but in order to do so, they had to get their passports updated in Guatemala. While at the

government offices, Adriana's mother found herself in
a predicament when she was required to show proof of
marriage. Her husband had left for the United States,
and thus, there would be no way to update her passport
in an honest manner. Thus, she went back home and
asked a member of the town to pretend to be her husband while in the government office. Adriana remembers a bitter indignation overwhelm her as her mother
lied to the government officers. The anger stemmed
from her father's absence and her mother's fib. Once
the passports were updated, Adriana and her family
said their goodbyes before heading off on the plane to
Texas against the pleas of her extended family. Her great
grandmother was hurt most by the ordeal as she was
unlikely to ever see Adriana again.

When Adriana, her mother, and her baby brother arrived in Texas, they had problems navigating their way
to New Jersey. They stayed in a hotel for a few days, and
Adriana remembers going down to the small pool on
the property. Adriana was not involved in the talks her
mother had with the local citizens, but they were eventually allowed to stay with a family in Texas for a few days
before going to Los Angeles, where there were buses that
could take them to New Jersey. Adriana remembers the
long trail of seashells outside of the Texans' house. She
grabbed a few of them to bring to her father once they
reunited. In Texas, they paid a stranger to drive them
to Los Angeles. Adriana notes the apparently drunken
nature of the man, and although she does not know for

sure if the man was under the influence, she did remember that his driving nearly killed them.

They took multiple rests on the side of the road, and at one point, there was a downpour. The baby was drenched as they rushed to the car, the biting cold November temperatures worsening his state. The eight-month-old baby came down with a fever, and with no medicine, Adriana's mother urged the erratic driver to hasten their trip to Los Angeles, where medical staff could treat him appropriately. Adriana recalls her mothers' state of stark trepidation as her baby was on the verge of death. Adriana's mother constantly prayed during the car ride to Los Angeles for her newborn's health. Once they arrived, Adriana's mother immediately took the baby to the emergency room, where he was given proper medical treatments and was diagnosed with the flu.

While in Los Angeles, they knocked on the doors of different families to see who would take them in. Someone eventually opened their doors to Adriana and her family, though she soon found out that these people, who looked like cowboys to a young Adriana, partied all night, incessantly drinking and blasting music from speakers. They did, however, help Adriana's mother with the baby by giving him food and medicine to treat his flu.

After a few days of staying with the "cowboys" in Los Angeles, Adriana, her mother, and her brother took busses across the country to get to New Jersey.

Adriana recalls passing through Las Vegas and seeing the beautiful lights, an awesome sight that stood in stark contrast to her homeland in Guatemala. Following multiple transfers from bus to bus, her mother repeatedly waking her up from her sleep, snow began to fall from the sky. Adriana had never seen snow, as the hot climate of Guatemala had prevented the strange new form of precipitation. The snow in the eyes of a five-year-old was a marvelous sight until the bus broke down. They were stranded in the cold for hours, and Adriana's mother was worried that her baby would again fall victim to sickness. Fortunately, the baby never contracted any disease, and once they arrived in New Jersey, Adriana's father was there to embrace them.

While in New Jersey, problems arose with the logistics of housing. Adriana, her mother, and her brother could not live with the father in the same apartment because the room he paid for could not house four people. Instead, Adriana's mother had to contact her best friend, who could only support the three of them. Thus, for the few months they lived in New Jersey, Adriana and her family were separated from the person they traveled across the country to reunite with. Adriana's mother enrolled her daughter in the American school systems, which would act as Adriana's first exposure to formal education. The class was bilingual, yet Adriana distinctly recalls being teased for her lack of proper English skills. The foreign language was the most difficult adjustment for Adriana, but her elders reassured her that her young age would make the language easier to learn.

Adriana's parents were concerned about their divided lives, and after a few months, Adriana's mother contacted her cousin, who was living in New York. Adriana eventually moved in with her aunt, and although the apartment was small, the family could live together. Adriana's aunt could also provide her father with a job so that they could stabilize themselves and find their own apartment.

In New York, Adriana was enrolled in another school, which was also bilingual. The teacher, however, constantly berated her for her lack of proper English skills. Adriana felt humiliated, which affected her disposition at home. She was frustrated when her peers began to bully her just as before, following the example of the teacher. For a time, Adriana wanted to return to Guatemala, where she could speak without being confronted by the incessant hurtful laughter of her peers. She also missed her extended family, which contributed to her precarious mental state. Adriana's mother pulled her out of school in Kindergarten, and in the first grade, she was placed in a new school. Adriana remembers meeting her best friend, who was from the Philippines and did not speak English either. They communicated using hand signals and facial expressions. Over the years, Adriana picked up English, but she was still bullied for having an accent when speaking the language. One day in the third grade, she returned from school with a piercing headache. She sobbed for hours, but she never told her mother why she was upset. She did not want to be transferred to another school. Her mother recognized the problem and immediately took action. She drove to the school in a fury the very next day and complained to the teacher, demanding the teasing end.

Familial tensions festered while living in the apartment with her aunt and uncle. Adriana's father was working for her uncle on her mother's side as a mechanic. Adriana's mother and her aunt constantly argued over their conflicting idiosyncrasies. According to Adriana, her uncle also took advantage of her father by not paying him properly for his work. Adriana had never met her mother's cousin before life in New York, and the constant arguments left a bad impression on her. They eventually moved out of her apartment and stayed with an Ecuadorian lady, who was kind enough to house them. Adriana's father found a job at an auto shop where his friend was working. Adriana understood the financial pressures her family was subject to, and thus, she never made materialistic requests to her parents.

Adriana's father wanted to get his drivers' license in Maryland, and she remembers having a vivid dream the night before he took the trip that the police stopped him. She was worried for her father's safety, and throughout the day during her classes, she was concerned that he would not return home. When Adriana's mother picked her up from school, her mother told her that her father was stopped by the police. She was in a state of utter shock, for her dream was a vision. Her mother was furious as to why her daughter did not tell her about the vision. Adriana's mother said she would have prayed for her father had she known of the premonition.

Fortunately, her father was only stopped by the police and given a warning. That night, however, Adriana's mother told her husband she wanted to go back to Guatemala. She was frightened by living in a country where she could be deported at any moment, and she was still having difficulty adjusting to the language in the new country. The financial burden of living in the nation was taxing as well as their apartment was draining their ability to live fruitful lives. In the next few weeks, they bought four tickets to go back to Guatemala. Adriana and her family packed their luggage and were prepared to leave the following day. Adriana's mother, however, made an astounding proposal. She exclaimed that if they could find a cheaper apartment in the next twenty-four hours that could support their family, they would stay in the United States. Adriana notes that by God's grace, they found a three-bedroom apartment that they could afford. The family canceled their plans and vowed to be more cautious around police officers and government officials.

Medical difficulties frequently plagued Adriana's family during times of celebration. The morning of Adriana's eighth-grade graduation, her brother began to throw up in the living room, so her parents took him to the emergency room, where his appendix had to be removed. While her mother and father were at the hospital, Adriana graduated with only her aunt and her best friend watching her. After the graduation ceremony, she rushed to the hospital to console her family. A year later, when Adriana was fourteen years old and planning her fifteenth birthday, also known as a quinceañera, she became very sick. She had abdominal pains and was diagnosed with gallbladder disease. She described the next two weeks as one of the most hectic experiences of her life. She was not able to walk, and her parents did not know whether or not to cancel the festivities. Luckily, her symptoms resolved, and she was able to celebrate the important milestone.

When the Dream Act came out, Adriana was only ten years old. At the time, she did not understand the significance of the act, but when she turned fifteen, her mother told her that she needed to get registered so that she could work and get a drivers' license. Adriana was always aware of the restrictions placed on her from a young age, and the day of her fifteenth birthday, she went to a lawyer's office and applied for DACA. When she received confirmation of her status as a dreamer from the United States government, she remembers being ecstatic. Her family joyously celebrated her home in the United States. Although she always considered America to be her homeland, she had often felt like a second-class citizen. Registering as a dreamer was a significant step in making Adriana feel welcome in the country she grew up in.

When she began the college application process,

Adriana applied for an American Dream Scholarship, which was for intelligent dreamers looking for a college education in the United States but who were unable to pay for the cost of college. The scholarship would cover all four years of college. For weeks, she and her mother would refine the application for the scholarship, and although Adriana never thought she would receive the money, her hopes were realized. That night, her family ardently celebrated Adriana and her achievements.

Aside from constant bullying stemming from her imperfect language skills in the United States, Adriana faced other forms of more blatant discrimination while in the country. One time, when Adriana was in a bank, she was speaking to the lady working at the front desk in Spanish. Another woman entered the bank, and exclaimed, "This is America! Learn how to speak English."

Adriana responded in a calm manner, stating, "The second most spoken language in America is Spanish."

The woman was in shock since she thought Adriana was only capable of speaking Spanish. She responded, "Oh, you speak very good English."

Adriana eventually received her cosmetology license while in high school and graduated with honors. In order to afford her college education, Adriana needed to work part-time. She started working at LL Bean as her first job, where she worked for two years after classes. She also worked at a salon every Saturday doing nails. Adriana emphasizes her academic focus despite her busy schedule. She enjoyed keeping herself occupied with multiple jobs and schoolwork. She will be graduating from college in two years.

Recently, Adriana applied for an internship as an accountant, which she plans on pursuing as a career. The main facets of her life right now revolve around work, school, and church. Her parents have wanted to return to Guatemala for quite some time now, but they were waiting to attain the necessary funds to build a stable life in Guatemala. Adriana notes that her parents were waiting for their son to graduate high school, and after that, they would decide whether or not they would stay in the United States. Adriana emphasizes the main reason her parents wanted to return to Guatemala is that their extended family still resided in the country. The separation between Adriana's family and the extended family in Guatemala was a challenge for her parents, and since Adriana was only five years of age when she left for the United States, she does not have as much of a connection with her family in Guatemala as compared to her parents.

Adriana's journey to the United States at such a young age was fueled by her mother's fighting spirit. She brought her two young children, one of whom was an infant, to the United States in the hopes she could reunite with her husband. The difficult adjustments Adriana had to face were met with discriminatory practices, often due to her flawed English skills. Despite the challenges her family faced financially and socially, Adriana persevered and has made significant and impressive progress toward the American dream through education and government aid, and although her family's future is uncertain, Adriana's wealth of experience, holding multiple jobs at once, provide her with a solid foundation upon which to build a beautiful life moving forward.

EPILOGUE

Hope can drive people halfway across the world to a land where they are not welcomed by all. Most people in the United States notice immigrants' presence in society, either through news broadcasts or by seeing them on the street. Not many, however, listen to their struggles and experiences. These stories exemplify the burdensome nature of a journey to the United States. Some faced the pinnacle of their struggles in their home country. Others realized the most challenging realities on the journey to America. Some confronted the greatest difficulties while in the United States, the very country they aspired to reside in. Perhaps the immigrants' featured in this book have yet to encounter their most overwhelming experiences. The beautiful facet of these stories is that they all share in a common theme: none of them are done being written.

The United States is at a turning point. Immigrants are at the forefront of national politics and local debate, but for all the chaotic screams on our television screens, in our newspapers, and on our social media, not many listen to the very people fueling the discussion. Instead, people who claim to be experts on the issue simultaneously spew judgment and propose policy solutions. Their opinions may well be valid, but in order to be truly be informed, one must listen to the actual fears, hopes, and day-to-day struggles these people face. There are millions of undocumented immigrants in the United States, yet in the mainstream, their voices are in the shadows, silenced by government intimidation.

These stories have not only changed my perspective on how we should approach the immigration debate, but they have also shifted my views on the struggles of these people. Undocumented immigrants choose to travel to America for a variety of reasons, but they all come in search of a better life. Those interviewed in this book were economic immigrants, asylum seekers, political dissidents, and dreamers. The common thread in this diverse group of people from different home countries, genders, ages, and financial backgrounds was a willingness to persevere and a deep love of family. The same reasons that brought my grandparents from Argentina fifty years ago are the reasons immigrants continue to journey to the United States today. People rarely realize these brilliant facets of undocumented immigrants in America, and debates surrounding immigration should always keep their humanity and their voices in mind.

Before embarking on this literary endeavor, I had never had the opportunity to converse with an undocumented immigrant. Despite their pivotal role in our culture, most citizens have never spoken to these wonderful people. I was surprised to find so many volunteers with such vibrant stories living within my small community. Many conveyed their appreciation for what I was doing, and I am truly grateful for the stories they shared with me. Their journeys will always stay with me, and I hope I am not the last native-born citizen they share their experiences with. Their voices are an integral step toward a more understanding society.

ACKNOWLEDGMENTS

Thank you **Mr. Stephen Mounkhall** for being my mentor over the years. This project was made possible by your personal advice, creative suggestions, guiding voice, weekly meetings and overall generous use of your time and wisdom, even during the summer months.

Thank you **Ms. Jennifer Rosenzweig** for allowing me to interview many of your students from your English language classes. The majority of the immigrants in this book came from your class, and I am grateful for that opportunity.

Thank you **Mr. Christopher Paulison** for helping me find research on the struggles of undocumented immigrants in America and for helping me prepare my pitch to immigrant organizaions.

Thank you **Ms. Carol D'Angelo** for checking over my English to Spanish translations for my interview questions and legal release forms.

Thank you **Mr. Jeremy Szerlip** for helping me prepare my pitch to immigrant organizations.

Thank you **Ms. Kami Wright** for helping me find the legal release forms to ensure anonymity for the immigrants.